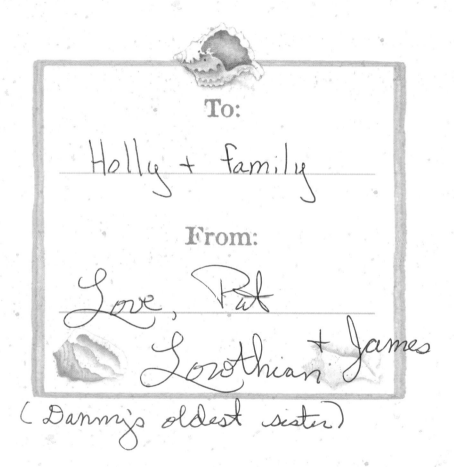

To:

Holly + family

From:

Love, Pat
Lorothian + James

(Danny's oldest sister)

Acknowledgments

To my sister, Bobbie Wilkinson, for your tireless efforts,
your editorial assistance, your generous spirit,
and for sharing my dream so completely...

To my colleagues in the National Speakers Association, for your
constant friendship, advice, and support...

To my relatives and friends who have stood by me over the years and
given me unfailing love and support...

To the many who were strong enough to share their brokenness with me...

To my new "family" at Alive Communications and Harvest House
Publishers, for believing in me and in my message...

And to the Lord, for His constant inspiration, guidance,
and unconditional love...

Thank you all for making this book possible.

Dedication

To my parents, Mae and Newt Hamblet, for giving me life, love,
my passion for the ocean, and my greatest gift, my faith.

To my husband, Steve, for sharing my life...for your inspiration,
love, and total support of all my dreams.

To Todd, Kevin, and Kristin, my greatest treasures, for making
me the proudest and luckiest mom in the world.

In loving memory of Emily and Rog Adams, two of
my life's richest blessings.

And in memory of those lost on September 11, 2001...
to their families...to the heroic men and women
who risk their lives daily to help us live in
safety and freedom. God bless you all.

My Beautiful Broken Shell

*Words of Hope to
Refresh the Soul*

Carol Hamblet Adams

Paintings by
D. Morgan

HARVEST HOUSE™ PUBLISHERS

EUGENE, OREGON

My Beautiful Broken Shell
Text copyright © 1998 by Carol Hamblet Adams
Published by Harvest House Publishers
Eugene, Oregon 97402

Library of Congress Cataloging-in-Publication Data

Adams, Carol Hamblet, 1943-
  My beautiful broken shell/Carol Hamblet Adams; illustrations by D. Morgan.
    p. cm.
  Originally published: Bloomington, MN: Garborg's, c1998.
  ISBN 0-7369-0870-6
    1. Consolation. I. Morgan, D. II. Title.
  BV4905.3 .A33 2002
  248.8'6--dc21
                                    2001051582

Published in association with the literary agency of Alive Communications, Inc., 7680 Goddard
Street, Suite 200, Colorado Springs, CO 80920.

Carol Hamblet Adams is a writer and motivational speaker who has had a life-long love of the ocean.
She lives in Southeastern Massachusetts and on the Cape and gives keynote addresses, seminars, and
retreats. She can be reached at P.O. Box 1234, Attleboro, MA 02703, or at carol@carolhambletadams.com.

Artwork appearing in this book is copyrighted by Doris Morgan and may not be reproduced
without the artist's permission. To learn more about the D. Morgan collector's club or to locate
a preferred dealer near you, please contact her exclusive print publisher and distributor, Cottage
Garden Collections, toll-free at 1-877-210-3456.

Design and production by Koechel Peterson and Associates, Inc., Minneapolis, Minnesota.

Printed in China.

05 06 07 08 09 10 11 / IM / 20 19 18 17 16 15 14

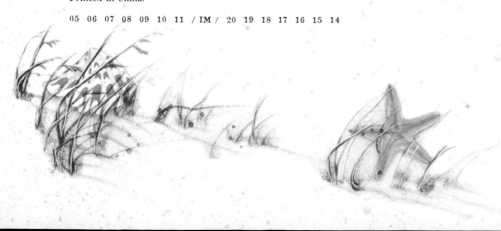

I'm so grateful for the peace and the
calm of the seashore, where time stands
still and unrushed...where I can see and
feel the beauty all around me.

This is my first morning at the ocean,
and as I walk to the beach, feeling
the rich, warm sand beneath my feet,
I decide to collect a few shells.

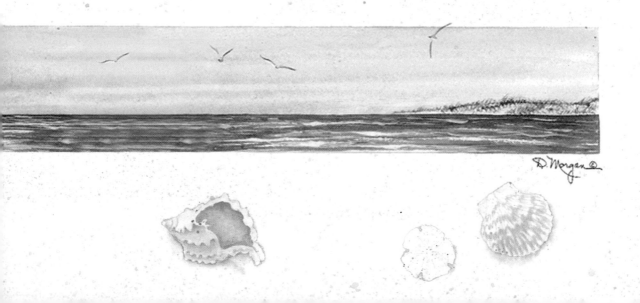

It is low tide and I watch, mesmerized, as the ocean rises slowly...curls...and then spills its white-laced foam onto the shore.

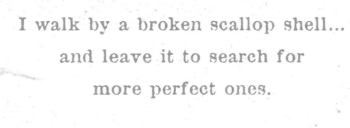

I walk by a broken scallop shell...
and leave it to search for
more perfect ones.

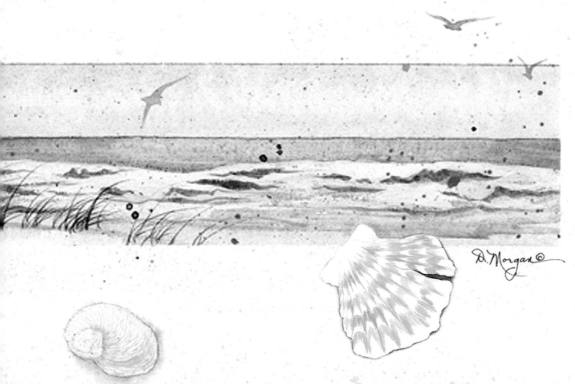

D. Morgan ©

$\mathcal{B}$ut then I stop...
go back...and pick up
the broken shell. I realize
that this shell is me
with my broken heart.

This shell is people who are hurting...
people who have lost loved ones...
people who are frightened or alone...
people with unfulfilled dreams.

This shell has had to fight so hard to
keep from being totally crushed by the
pounding surf...just as I have had to.

Yet this shell is still out on
the beautiful sandy shore...
just as I am.

Thank You, Lord, that I haven't
been completely crushed by the
heaviness in my heart...by the
pounding of the surf.

If our world were only filled with perfect
shells, we would miss some of life's most
important lessons along the way.
We would never learn from adversity...
from pain...from sorrow.

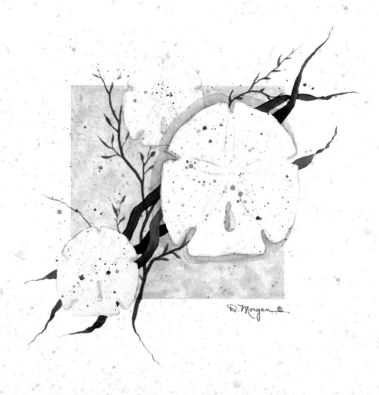

D. Morgan ©

Thank You, Lord, for all that I learn from my brokenness...for the courage it takes to live with my pain...and for the strength it takes to remain on the shore.

$\mathscr{B}$roken shells teach us not to
look at our imperfections...but to look
at the beauty...the great beauty...
of what is left.

If anything is still left of me or my loved ones, then that is enough to grab hold of...to keep me going... to thank God for.

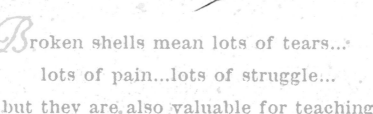

*B*roken shells mean lots of tears...
lots of pain...lots of struggle...
but they are also valuable for teaching
faith, courage, and strength.

Broken shells inspire others
and demonstrate the will to go on
in a way that no perfect shell
could ever do.

Broken shells are shells
that have been tested...
and tried...and hurt...
yet they don't quit.
They continue to be.

D. Morgan

*Thank You, Lord, for the great
strength it takes to simply be...
even when I hurt so deeply that there
seems to be nothing left of me.*

As I walk along the beach picking up
shells, I see that each one has its own
special beauty...its own unique pattern.

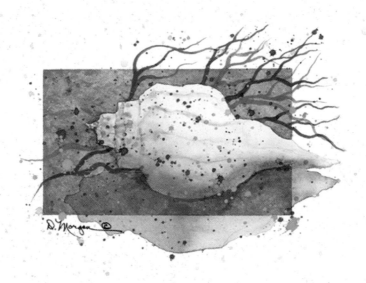

Lord, help me to see my own
beautiful pattern...and to remember
that each line and each color on
my shell was put there by You.

*Help me not to compare myself
to others, so that I may
appreciate my own uniqueness.*

*Help me to truly accept
myself just as I am,
so that I may sing
the song in my heart...
for no one else has
my song to sing...
my gift to give.*

I watch the rolling surf
toss new shells onto the shore,
and I am reminded of the many times
that I, too, have been tossed
by the storms of life and worn down
by the sands of time, just like
my beautiful broken shell.
But I am reminded that broken
shells don't stand alone.

D. Morgan©

*T*hank **You**, Lord, for being with me
to share my life...to help me
carry my burdens.

Thank You for the precious gift of faith
that keeps me strong when I am weak...
that keeps me going when it
would be easier to quit.

Thank You, Lord, for hope in times of despair...
for light in times of darkness...
for patience in times of suffering...
for assuring me that with You
all things are possible.

A wave crashes, sending tiny sand crabs
scurrying for safety...and I am reminded
that even the smallest creatures depend
on each other. Especially in our brokenness,
we need the Lord...and we need one another.

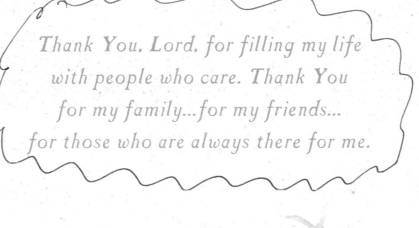

*Thank You, Lord, for filling my life
with people who care. Thank You
for my family...for my friends...
for those who are always there for me.*

D. Morgan ©

As I look at my beautiful broken shell,
I see that it has nothing to hide.
It doesn't pretend to be perfect or whole...
its brokenness is clear for everyone to see.

*Lord, may I be strong enough
to show my pain and brokenness
like this shell. May I give myself
permission to hurt...to cry...to be human.*

D. Morgan ©

May I have the courage to risk
sharing my feelings with others
so that I may receive support
and encouragement along the way.

Lord, help me to reach out to others....
especially to the broken and discouraged...
not only to love them but to learn
from them as well.

May I listen...comfort...
and give unconditional love to
all who pass my way.

D. Morgan

Lord, help me realize that
I am not the only one hurting...
that we all have pain in our lives.
Help me remember that in
my brokenness I am still whole
and complete in Your sight.

D. Morgan®

As I walk among the many washed-up shells,
I suddenly spot a broken conch shell...
white and ordinary on the outside...
yet brilliant coral inside.

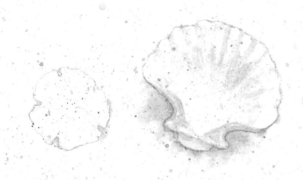

Lord, help me see inside the hearts
of the people who touch my life...
and to see their true colors.

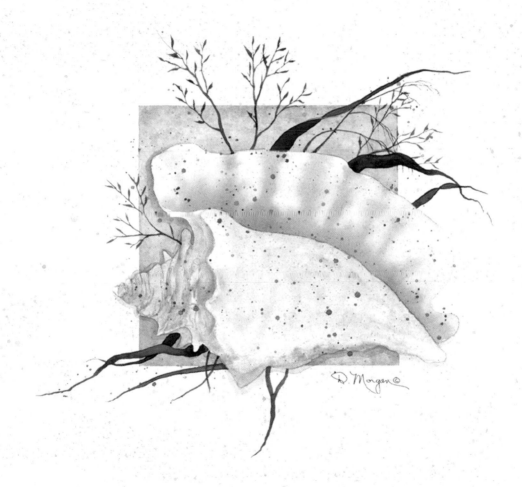

D. Morgan ©

Somehow, here at the ocean,
I receive so many gifts.
I am grateful for the inner peace
that fills my soul.

I take time to notice sandpipers
playing along the shore...
beach grasses swaying in the salty breezes.
I delight in finding simple treasures...
a piece of smooth green glass
polished by the waves...
a transparent white stone...
a starfish.

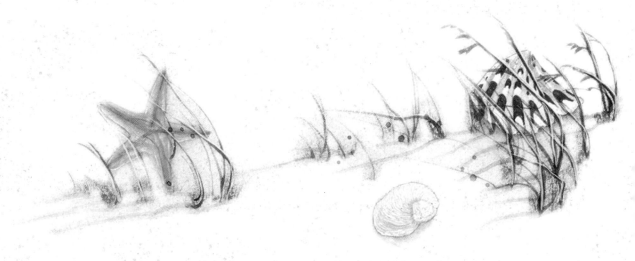

Lord, help me to remain childlike in
my appreciation for life. Please slow me down...
that I may always see the extraordinary in the ordinary.
That I may always wonder at the shell in the sand...
the dawn of a new day...the beauty of a flower...
the blessing of a friend...the love of a child.

In my brokenness, may I never take
life so seriously that I forget to
laugh along the way.

May I always take the time to watch
a kite dance in the sky...to sing...
to pick daisies...to love...to take risks...
to believe in my dreams.

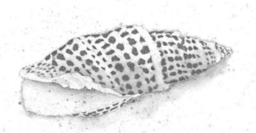

As I look once more at the broken
scallop shell in my hand, I am
reminded of all the beautiful shells
God has placed around me.

Lord, may I truly value every moment
spent with my loved ones while
this life is so briefly mine.

*Let me not destroy the beauty of today
by grieving over yesterday...
or worrying about tomorrow.*

May I cherish and appreciate
my shell collection each and every day...
for I know not when the tide will come
and wash my treasures away.

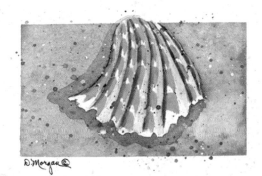

Thank You, Lord, for embracing my shell...
whether I am whole or broken.
Thank You for sending me loved ones who care.
Thank You for holding me in the palm of Your hand...
for keeping me safe from the pounding surf.

For now,
I'll just continue walking
and add to my collection
of beautiful shells.

D. Morgan®